DIGITAL AND INFORMATION LITERACY ™

NETIQUETTE
A STUDENT'S GUIDE TO DIGITAL ETIQUETTE
REVISED AND UPDATED

KATHY FURGANG

rosen publishing's
rosen central ®

New York

Published in 2018 by The Rosen Publishing Group, Inc.
29 East 21st Street, New York, NY 10010

Copyright © 2018 by The Rosen Publishing Group, Inc.

First Edition

Library of Congress Cataloging-in-Publication Data

Names: Furgang, Kathy, author.
Title: Netiquette : a student's guide to digital etiquette / Kathy Furgang.
Description: New York : Rosen Central, 2018. | Series: Digital and information literacy | Includes bibliographical references and index. | Audience: Grades 5–8.
Identifiers: LCCN 2017023105| ISBN 9781499439137 (library bound) | ISBN 9781499439113 (pbk.) | ISBN 9781499439120 (6 pack)
Subjects: LCSH: Online etiquette—Juvenile literature.
Classification: LCC TK5105.878 .B38 2017 | DDC 395.5—dc23
LC record available at https://lccn.loc.gov/2017023105

Manufactured in China

CONTENTS

INTRODUCTION

Teens and young people nowadays navigate an entirely different world than their counterparts did just twenty to thirty years ago. It was once tough enough to navigate new social situations as an adolescent, dealing with peers, adults, authority figures, and society at large. Modern youth have to deal with these things in real life (IRL) and online simultaneously. Each sphere bleeds into the other, and it has made coming of age more complicated than ever.

When people think of the proper and respectful ways to behave in society and in company, they think of the word "etiquette." Etiquette comprises the mostly unwritten rules of how to interact with others. It helps people get along smoothly, and its successful execution prepares teens for entry into adult, polite society.

Different forms of etiquette apply to different situations. School has its own rules and rituals, and power dynamics between students, teachers, and administrators. A meeting at work or a gathering at a house of worship has entirely different rules. Meanwhile, while home etiquette might be more relaxed, in some families, etiquette is enforced or held in higher regard than others.

Online rules of etiquette—sometimes referred to by the recently coined expression "netiquette"—are both rooted in real-world etiquette and in some

Being social online is second nature to many people these days. Internet etiquette ("netiquette") can help young people navigate the often uncertain rules of behavior that a modern and wired life demands.

ways diverge dramatically. Still, netiquette's goals are the same as those of traditional etiquette: establishing a safe, pleasant, and civil setting for those who interact; in this case, to enjoy and thrive in online environments.

Thus, many activities that are frowned upon IRL are also discouraged on the internet, such as stealing, starting arguments or fights or otherwise acting in a bullying or aggressive manner, spreading rumors and/or engaging in gossip, and pretending to be someone else in a dishonest or disingenuous fashion.

The internet serves as a giant community with many smaller ones within it. Preserving it as a destination many people actually want to return to takes a group effort. Minding one's manners encourages others to do the same.

Of course, there is a great deal of negativity online. From serial harassers and predators, to anonymous trolls trying to get a rise out of anyone, to identity thieves and other dishonest actors, online spaces are not always the ideal communities we might hope them to be.

Netiquette means so much more than interacting politely. It also covers the correct protocols on how to use computers and other online devices, and how to access the internet in public, whether one is in a coffee shop, public area, school, or local library.

In addition, netiquette also refers to responsible online research—including avoiding plagiarism and attributing sources correctly. How does it apply to working together on school projects, where you might need to share computers or other resources? What about the rules that govern civility when you text or chat with your friends on a computer or smartphone in your spare time? All of the above tie into netiquette, which helps the online world go round.

Chapter 1

A Public Internet

hile many people own computers or other devices like smartphones and tablets, not everyone has their own internet access. In other cases, someone might need to use computers at school or in other public places—for example, for in-school projects, or as part of a computer class or lab. Chances are that even those fortunate enough to have their own computers need to share equipment at some point. Regardless, everyone should be aware of the rules governing equipment that everyone has to share.

Public Computers

When using public computer terminals, there is often a limit to the amount of time you are allowed to spend at a workstation. Check around for posted rules. You will often find that you have to provide identification and enter your name on a sign-up sheet before being allowed to use the computer. This allows the library or computer lab that owns the computers to track who

Some computer labs will have much of the equipment you need, including headphones. Others may require you to bring your own.

is using the different computer stations and who might be responsible for any problems that occur during the day.

Once you gain access to a computer workstation, you may have to log in with personal information such as your name, an identification number, and/or a password. Do not give too much information. You should not be asked for a social security number or credit card number when using a public computer. Basic, public-record information such as your address or telephone number should be enough information to identify you.

If there are time limits to computer workstation usage, come prepared to do work, especially if people are waiting. Zoning out can be counterproductive and may cause you to take more time than you need without your realizing it.

Aside from abiding by the general procedures governing public computer use, users should obey the specific time limits and the rules of the library or computer lab. Many libraries offer people a half-hour to an hour of computer time per session or day. Others allow you to sign up again and wait at the end of the line for another session.

If there are headphones available at the library, school, or computer lab (or you have your own), be sure to use them if you are going to be listening to music or playing any audio or video. It is rude to subject others to noise that may be distracting, whether they are working hard or simply relaxing. Make sure to leave borrowed headphones clean (preferably with antibacterial wipe) and in the same condition and working order you received them.

Many establishments will advertise prominently whether they provide Wi-Fi or not, and some may indicate that using it is free of charge. Other places may require that you purchase a food or drink before logging on.

There are often rules about downloading files on public computers. Sometimes you may be researching a topic for school and a website requires that you download a file onto your desktop to view it. However, check with the school, library, or computer lab workers to see if this is OK or if there is a designated place where you should be downloading these files instead. In addition, many public computers block the user from going to inappropriate websites.

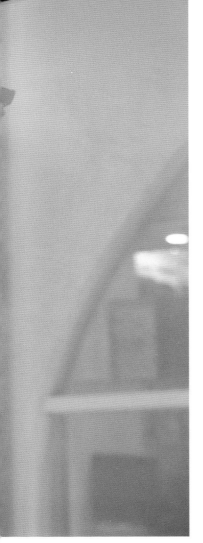

Places without time limits on public computer usage rely on users to follow the honor system. For example, someone who has finished their work should look around to see if others are waiting. Avoid extending your session with leisure pursuits such as random internet surfing. Finish up and sign off so the next person can use it.

Sharing Wi-Fi (Politely)

Many people who have laptop computers, smartphones, or tablets enjoy the convenience of using them in public places that offer internet connections. It's very common to encounter free Wi-Fi hotspots in libraries, hotels, stores, airports, or restaurants. The word Wi-Fi is short for "wireless fidelity" and refers to signals that come from a device called a wireless router. The router broadcasts a signal through the air. The signal allows multiple devices near the router to connect to the internet with no need for wires or cables. Such networks have become so common that it is easy to take your computer with you when you go out and easily find a place that provides internet access.

11

File　Edit　View　Favorites　Tools　Help

MOBILE PHONES, SMARTPHONES, AND TEXTING

Mobile Phones, Smartphones, and Texting

Cell phones can be a great convenience for the user, but they can also be a major irritation for those around that person. If you receive a call in a public place, take note of the noise level where you are. If you're on a playground or at a sports game, go ahead and chat away. But if you are in a bookstore, library, movie theater, or museum, take the call outside, let it go to voice-mail, or tell the caller you will get back to him or her later. Chances are the caller doesn't realize where you are, so it's not rude to let them know that you can't talk. Also, your cell phone should be in silent or vibrate mode in these kinds of public places.

Texting can be an alternative form of communication in places where speaking aloud is frowned upon or forbidden. However, do not text in movie theaters or at live performances, as phone LED light distracts other audience members and even performers, as does the sound of keys typing. One reason to cut down on or avoid texting altogether when out with company is that it can be rude. It also takes one away from experiencing real life in a fulfilling manner.

Many people view texting and talking on a phone as a sign of disrespect if the person they are out with does it too much. If you are in a restaurant with friends or family, think about turning your cell phone off or just replying to the texts later. The people you are with want to spend time with you and have your full attention. Many people have realized that constant stimulation from instantly communicating with others (including via social media), and obsessively surfing online while out with people are negative behaviors, and can even be addictive.

Common sense rules apply to using laptops in public. Pay attention to any time limits placed on Wi-Fi users or any fees that apply (not all Wi-Fi is free). Even when wireless connections are offered for free, that does not mean you should take unfair advantage of the place that is offering the service.

Try not to take up more space than you need. Don't take over an entire table that other customers may want to use. If you are in a café or eatery, order something to eat or drink. The establishment is in the business of selling food and drinks, not offering free internet service. Use headphones if you are going to be playing audio or video. The point is to be as discreet as possible when you are doing personal business in a public place. This refers not only to computer use, but also to the use of cell phones and other technologies.

Forgoing texting or talking on the cell phone is sometimes hard to do for young people. They have grown up with these technologies and do not view their use in social situations as annoying or rude. Many young people do not feel that they are being disrespected if a friend begins to talk to or text someone else when they are together. However, many other people do feel this way and it is important to have respect for everyone around you.

Refrain from Piggybacking

Most modern computers and devices can connect to the internet without wires. This means that people can take their computers anywhere they go and more often than not find a place that offers access to the internet via Wi-Fi. Before, online access happened only via cable or phone line connections, making the computer immobile. People had to remain at their home, school, library, or office desks to do their work. Wi-Fi has allowed computers and their users great mobility. Now they can connect to the internet in cafés, parks, hotel rooms and lobbies, trains, airports, and other public places.

Anyone who has gone online while out and about knows users have a list of such networks available in the immediate area. These connections change as you move from place to place. If you are in your own home, for example, you may check your network settings and see the Wi-Fi networks of

Using smartphones and other devices in cinemas has become such a problem that some movie chains have even imposed zero tolerance policies on their usage while movies are playing.

your neighbors as well as your own. You may be at a café and see the names of wireless connections from nearby stores or businesses. Most of these will have a picture of a padlock next to them to indicate that access to that router is protected by a password. People do this to protect their privacy. They paid for this connection and do not want strangers to log onto it and use it for free.

However, some people either do not know how to make their network private (password protected) or are not aware that it should be protected. Logging onto one of these unlocked Wi-Fi networks is called piggybacking. The person who has paid for the network connection is doing the digital equivalent of carrying you—giving you a free ride, in other words. Using this network without permission is, essentially, theft. In addition, when too many computers use one signal, it can slow the connection for everyone.

So when you are out in public, choose only free, unprotected networks. Some places that offer Wi-Fi access will have password-protected networks, but they will provide you with the code or password to get online when you ask. This allows them to make sure that only their customers are using the service, not freeloaders.

Chapter 2

Responsible Research

One of the most important developments for high school and academic research in general over the past twenty years has been the internet revolution. Few deny that the internet has been positive for students seeking knowledge, especially with the convenience of accessing it nearly anywhere—at school, at home, or out in public, all at the tap of a screen or mouse-click. While libraries are still vital parts of researching and learning, for students who live far from one or need to work after hours, the ease of online research is a tremendous help.

Copy-Paste Plagiarism

You have most likely learned how to compile a bibliography or make footnotes. These same citation rules apply to information you get off the internet. You can use internet-derived information to get facts and data, but the sources must be cited. As is the case with printed books and articles, you cannot copy the exact wording from an internet-based source and place it in your report without making it clear it is a quote and where it came from.

Taking good notes is important not only to get the needed information, but also to be able to cite all sources used in one's research accurately.

According to *USA Today*, many students are likely using information technology irresponsibly. A study reveals that eighty-three percent of undergraduate college students use the internet for their academic work. However, close to ninety percent of these students admit that they have seen their peers "at least sometimes" copy and paste information from the web without citing the source or paraphrasing the text (rewriting something in one's own words). It may be easy to do with just the click of a finger, but it is not ethical and not legal to do so with copyrighted content online (or off).

17

File   Edit   View   Favorites   Tools   Help

USING AUDIO AND VIDEO SOURCES

Using Audio and Video Sources

It is necessary to credit online audio and video clips used in presentations or referenced in one's sources for an essay or paper. Suppose you are giving a multimedia oral presentation to your class. You want to use music in the background and you also want to project a video on a screen that you downloaded from a NASA website. You can certainly do all of these things. Just make a list of the materials used and the websites you got them from. Submit a complete list of sources to your teacher, including the material's title, the website's name, the date of the material's creation, the date you downloaded it, and the URL.

Remember that you cannot download most music from the internet without paying for it. Most songs are protected by copyright laws. That means that the right to decide how a song gets used and distributed is up to the person who holds the copyright. In many cases, the artist holds the copyright and should receive payment when the works are downloaded and distributed over the web. If you own MP3s or other audio formats and want to use them in your multimedia report, it is fine to use these in class. The music has already been purchased, and you are not selling or distributing anything with the song on it. But you still must cite your sources by submitting a list of everything you have used in the creation of your presentation—books, magazines, articles, songs, video clips, and photos.

Missions · Galleries · NASA TV · Follow NASA · Downloads · About · NASA Audiences

Search

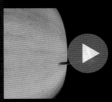

Space to Ground: American Recordholder: 04/28/2017

Cassini's First Dive Between Saturn and Its Rings

NASA VR: Cassini's Grand Finale (360 view)

President Trump Calls Space Station Crew on...

Earth Day 2017 - 4K Earth Views From Space

ScienceCasts: Close Approach Comets

Video clips—for example, of space program milestones on this NASA web page—are a great primary source. Research thoroughly how to cite these properly if you use them for projects or papers.

Copying and pasting in this manner is bound to backfire on student scholars. Students researching online to get work done as quickly as possible admit they are not truly learning or absorbing the content. They do not take the time to really sit and understand what they are reading. It

If you are having a hard time finding information for a project or paper, talk to your teacher or faculty advisor. This is preferable to resorting to plagiarism and having to face them after your actions have been discovered.

often takes time for the mind to absorb information. Quickly skimming text and then cutting and pasting it into a report accomplishes little. This kind of research technique shows only that you knew how to find the information.

The Fair Use Doctrine

Is simply citing the sources you use in your bibliography enough to allow you to use information from the internet? The Fair Use Doctrine says it is enough. This copyright rule is part of U.S. trademark law. It states that as long as the selection from the work you are reproducing (like a quote) is relatively short, you do not have to get written permission from the copyright holders to use it. This applies especially to using materials for educational purposes. So a student who quotes from a newspaper interview with the president of the United States does not need to obtain permission to use the material in his or her report. A song in a multimedia presentation can also be used without written permission from the copyright holder. However, that presidential interview or song should be listed in the project's bibliography.

MYTHS & FACTS

MYTH What I do online is my own private business.

FACT There are many laws regarding internet use, including those regarding harassment and threats in correspondence. The authorities may be alerted and may even impose penalties—including prison time—on those who threaten others or engage in other illegal online activities.

MYTH Cyberbullying only happens when someone threatens to hurt someone else and it can only happen on social networking sites.

FACT Insults and put-downs are also considered cyberbullying. Calling someone names online, even a friend, can be considered bullying. It can happen via email, text message, or through social networks and apps.

MYTH Etiquette doesn't matter that much when you are online, because it is "not the real world."

FACT These days, the distinction between "real life" and online barely exists, especially for young people who interact and socialize online as much as they do in person. Actions online can have serious real-world consequences.

Chapter 3

A Team Effort

Collaborative, or group, projects are common for young people in every grade. These days, there is little doubt that technology will be somehow involved, whether it is researching content, putting together reports, or presenting findings in a presentation. Group members need to approach sharing computers, devices, and other digital resources with respect and politeness. This is true for using computers at school or sharing laptops and other devices among each other while working on projects outside of school.

Keep in mind that a person's computer is a personal and private space. It should be treated as private property. If you go on a fellow student's device, by all means avoid opening documents, changing computer settings, reading emails, viewing photos, or copying a person's files—whether school-related or not—without their permission.

Etiquette on Email

When communicating online about a school report or project, keep it professional. Your teacher may ask to see your progress and sources. Imagine

Good etiquette, politeness, and kindness among group members on a school project will contribute to a fun and positive learning environment for everyone and will make your hard work feel lively and engaging.

how it would look if those sources were embedded in an email to a group member that also discussed group gossip, relationship troubles, or anything else you would consider a little too personal or damaging to your reputation or another person's.

As you write your emails regarding the group project, think about whom you are referring to in your correspondence. Are you mentioning any other students in the group? Be sure to add the email of any other person you are talking about in your email. This ensures that you will be careful and diplomatic about what you say about that person, and it also keeps them

File   Edit   View   Favorites   Tools   Help

CARBON COPY AND BLIND CARBON COPY

Carbon Copy and Blind Carbon Copy

The term CC stands for carbon copy. It is a term developed in the pre-computer and pre-photocopy era, when offices were not yet "paperless." When someone typed a letter on their typewriter and wanted to send copies of it to different people, they often used a piece of carbon paper. These purple carbon sheets were placed between two pieces of typing paper and rolled into the typewriter. When the person typed on the original, top sheet, an exact copy was printed on the second sheet beneath the carbon paper. The original copy would go to the person the letter is addressed to, and the carbon copy went to others not addressed in the letter. Anyone who received a carbon copy would be listed on the bottom of the letter, after the initials "CC."

Email offers a further technological wrinkle. The "BCC" option on email address lines stands for "Blind Carbon Copy." That means that a person receives a copy of the email, but none of the other recipients can see that person's email included on their end. The person's name and email address does not show up in the address fields.

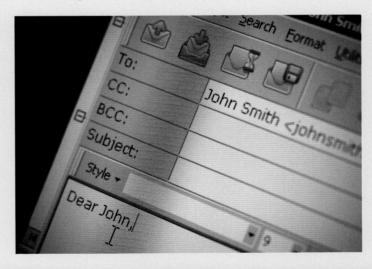

informed about your progress on the project. Don't refer to the other team members in a negative way, especially behind their back. Remember, you may be asked to show all your work on the project, including correspondence. It may be embarrassing for you and hurtful to the other student to see emails about a school project that portray him or her in a negative way.

Writing Formal Correspondence

Sometimes when working on a school project, you may want to correspond with someone from the community. Suppose you want to interview a local businessperson for a social studies, civics, or economics paper. Or maybe you want to invite a firefighter or a scientist to speak to your class as part of your project. You can talk with these people online and have a written record of the correspondence available for your teacher. This will help him or her better evaluate your work, level of involvement, and commitment to your project's success. There are some simple rules about using proper digital etiquette when conducting professional (non-personal) correspondence via email.

Just like a formal letter in print, official or formal email correspondence should have a greeting, a body, and a conclusion. The email will show the date, so you do not need to include that in the body of your letter. Your email should not include any internet shorthand or abbreviated spellings. Abbreviations such as "BTW" for "by the way," or "PLMK" for "please let me know," are fine between friends, but they are not appropriate in a business email. When writing emails, people often don't use correct punctuation, spelling, or capitalization. But this, too, is not appropriate for a business letter or a letter to someone you do not know well.

In addition to writing the letter in a professional manner, you must also give the person enough time to respond. If you are asking the person to visit your classroom or be interviewed next week, be sure to send the email as soon as possible. Not everyone checks their email every day, so you want to give them time to read it and consider your offer. It would be insulting if you

A well written letter that conveys clearly what you want will be more likely to attract a coveted guest speaker to your classroom.

emailed someone asking them to give a talk the next day or even the day after tomorrow. People have busy lives and their time is valuable, so be respectful and give them plenty of advance notice.

Your letter should also provide as much information as possible about the project and what you hope they can contribute to it so they do not need to ask you a lot of questions. If the person does not respond within a couple of days, send a friendly follow-up letter. If you are turned down, send a polite thank-you email for their time and consideration. Keep in mind that you may have to have a backup plan for your project if the person is unable to help. If the person does respond favorably, be sure to thank the person for their time and effort both before and after their participation.

Identifying Sources

When you are writing the bibliography for a project you did with a group, look at each source. Think about whether you actually used that book as a source of information that made it into or somehow informed your report. Did you do the research, or did another person in your group do it? If the project has a group credit, which means it was researched and written by the whole group, it may be fine if you are not familiar with all the sources that were referred to and used. But if you are responsible for writing your own paper, you should know exactly how and when you used each source that appears in the bibliography.

One of the things you should include in your bibliography entries is the date that you accessed the internet article. You may find that another person in your group used the same article, but he or she may have accessed it on a different day. Some websites are updated daily or weekly, so your partner may have downloaded a revised article or one that was not as current as yours. Be as accurate as you can with your recordkeeping.

TEN GREAT QUESTIONS
TO ASK A SCHOOL LIBRARIAN

1 Why does my teacher make us use different media formats to give our presentations in school?

2 How can I use a computer to prepare or give a presentation at school?

3 Is the information I get online better than the research I can get from books?

4 I do not have a computer at home, but I have a big research paper to do. How can I get extra time at a school computer?

5 My parents have not given me permission to use computers with the internet while I am at school, so I cannot do my research paper online. How else can I find digital information?

6 What should I do if the school computer blocks sites that I need to use in a school report and I do not have a computer at home?

7 How can I save my research and work on my paper if I do not have a computer at home?

8 What should I do if I want to send my teacher a file but he or she cannot open it?

9 How would someone know if the files I downloaded for a multimedia report were done legally or not?

10 How can I tell if the information I get online is accurate?

Chapter 4

Cyberbullying and Home Netiquette

opefully, home is a place where most students feel comfortable and casual. It is important to remember that the online world has seeped into all the different, and many formerly private, parts of our lives nowadays. It is important to take precautions and to make adjustments to stay both safe and sane. Many parents will make some effort to protect their kids from online dangers, but teens who have far more freedom in the digital realm should take extra care, too.

It is important to understand the rules of digital etiquette in order to remain safe from very real trouble in the so-called virtual world. Being familiar with digital etiquette will also help you recognize when someone is not following these important rules and trying to get you into trouble. Avoid communicating with these people. When someone else is not following these rules, it is important to let a trusted adult know. By following these rules, they can avoid the most common and also the most dangerous ways that people take advantage of the anonymity offered by the internet, avoid or correct poor netiquette, and help protect themselves and other members of their online communities.

Approaching the online world with enthusiasm and common-sense caution at the same time will make it more likely that your internet experiences will be positive ones.

Dealing With Cyberbullying

Cyberbullying is the use of digital technologies to express deliberate, repeated, and hostile behaviors toward others. It can happen in email, text messages, instant messages, blogs, or chat rooms in a private or a public format. Social networking sites such as Facebook and Twitter have become places where bullying occasionally occurs among students and other young people.

A random ten-year sampling of American middle and high school students by the Cyberbullying Research Center revealed that a big percentage of youth had experienced cyberbullying at some point. In May 2007, about 19 percent of respondents claimed to have been cyberbullied. By August 2016, that number had increased to about 34 percent.

Those numbers may be even higher since many teens are afraid to admit and report their harassment. They may feel that the problems will worsen if they draw attention to it. Sometimes they are embarrassed that they are being targeted or that people may not like them. But the best way to stop a problem is to address it directly and do something about it. It is best to cut of all contact with the bully, both in person and electronically, if possible. It is important to involve a trusted adult in the problem. Even minor cases of cyberbullying can affect a person's well-being, making it difficult to go online, study or do homework, or even go about their daily lives. Severe cases of cyberbullying can lead to victims taking their own lives and have sparked violent cases of retribution.

Getting Too Personal

Some people send photos or videos of themselves to friends. These images are meant for those friends' eyes only and may not be something they'd want anyone else to see. They may also send emails that are very private in nature or tell off-color jokes. Though meant as an inside joke or to be amusing in a private way, these images and words would be inappropriate if they somehow were viewed by someone other than the intended recipient.

There is no reason to feel shame about facing abuse, including cyberbullying, online. You will be surprised how much better you feel if you confide in someone you trust, such as a parent.

Other people, including classmates and strangers, may get their hands on these words and images, spread them around, and misuse them.

Many young people do not realize that once their images and words are sent, the digital information can be passed on or posted over the internet to a large group of people without their permission. Many times, students do not realize that, although they may trust their friend now, it is possible that they may not be able to trust him or her in the future. In addition, the inappropriate depiction of underage people below the age of 18 in photos or on video is illegal. This type of depiction is called pornography.

Also be cautious about posting overly personal, private, or inappropriate content on your blog, website, or social networking site. Not only do you have limited control (at best) over who can view this material, it will also continue to exist on the web long after you post it—and probably long after you come to regret it. This means that future boyfriends or girlfriends, college admissions officers, employers, law enforcement, and government agents will all be able to find this content if they wish to conduct a search on you for any reason. Once you put it out there, it's very hard, if not impossible, to reel it back in. A good rule of thumb is not to post any images or words that you wouldn't want your grandparents, potential future in-laws, or future bosses to see.

Beware of Online Predators

An internet predator is someone who uses email, dating sites, online ads, social networking sites, and other online portals to make contact with people for the purpose of harming them. A predator may want to rob, deceive, abduct, or attack a person physically or sexually. One in five teenagers in the U.S. who use the internet regularly say that they have received unwanted sexual offers online. This means someone has contacted them without invitation and tried to talk about sex, ask personal questions about sex and sexuality, or arrange a face-to-face meeting to have sex. Unfortunately, only 25 percent of these teens told a parent or trusted adult about it.

To avoid internet predators, refrain from talking to people online that you do not know. Never give away personal information to anyone, including name, address, phone number, and other identifying data. From the safe invisibility of the keyboard, internet predators often present themselves as someone your own age or as someone who is a friend of a friend of yours. They may even impersonate someone you know and trust. You must always remain vigilant when communicating on the internet and not be taken in by predators and imposters. If you make a date to meet a friend or acquaintance via email, text message, or on a social network, be sure to double up another communication channel (an actual phone call is best, so you hear their voice)

Arranging to meet someone you met online is a risky proposition to begin with. Under no circumstances should you agree to meet anyone by yourself in a remote place, as you never know what can happen.

so you know for sure that you've been communicating with the real person and not someone posing as him or her.

Flaming

The word flaming refers to the hostile or insulting interactions that people can have on the internet. People tend to say things on the internet that they wouldn't feel comfortable saying in person. People tend to feel more comfortable expressing anger, disgust, or disapproval in written form over the internet. Leaving comments on someone's Facebook or Twitter page that is rude or insulting is not good netiquette.

People often engage in flaming on blogs, chat rooms, message boards, or other sites where people are invited to post reviews of consumer products, music, movies, or books. Strangers can get into arguments in these discussion threads, with an unlimited number of people able to view them. Sometimes, once one aggressive user attacks someone who has posted a comment he or she disagrees with, other users feel emboldened to join in and gang up on the flaming victim.

Even if you have a username that does not reveal your real name—and you should choose a non-identifying username—this kind of harassment can make the internet an unpleasant place for everyone. It can make people

Being the target of cyberbullying or any other kind of malicious activity online, including internet pile-ons by friends or strangers, can be intensely alienating. This is another reason to seek immediate help.

hesitant to express an opinion, engage in intelligent and heartfelt conversation, or even venture onto the internet at all. The atmosphere created by flamers is very much like that created by schoolyard bullies. They turn what should be supportive and stimulating environments into ones poisoned by anger, dread, intimidation, fear, and ultimately, silence. Just as you would try to be civil to a person you talk with in person, have the same kind of respect for people online.

Do not hide behind the idea that what you are posting is anonymous because people do not know you or your real name. Think about what you are posting. Would you be willing to deliver this message to the person face-to-face? We must all do our part to create a safe and welcoming cyber-community. Just as you would try to be a good neighbor in your town or in your school, it is also your responsibility to be a good citizen in cyberspace. Think about whether the statement you are posting is something you would like to read about yourself. If you are in an argument with a friend, think twice before you post something nasty on his or her Facebook page. Just think of what it would be like if all of your friends, family, classmates, and acquaintances read unflattering things about you on your personal page.

"Do Unto Others . . ."

Keep in mind this ancient and ever-reliable recommendation, as relevant in the twenty-first century as it was in the first century: do unto others as you would have them do unto you. All of the principles and guidelines of netiquette—as they relate to public use of computers and electronic devices, academic research, group projects, and business and personal communication—are encapsulated in this timeless golden rule. It will always steer you right, whether in the real world or the virtual one.

GLOSSARY

BCC Short for blind carbon copy, an email function that allows copies of a message to be sent to others without anyone else seeing their email addresses in the correspondence.

CC Short for carbon copy, a function of email that allows for multiple recipients to receive a copy of a message.

collaborative Refers to efforts or projects done by a team or group.

copyright The legal right to publish works or perform art, and the right to allow others to do so.

cyberbullying Using digital technologies to engage in deliberate, repeated, and hostile or intimidating behavior towards others.

digital etiquette Unwritten rules about how to behave while using personal technology devices.

etiquette A set of rules helping to outline polite ways to behave in society.

Fair Use U.S. law that states that copyright material may be used without permission or payment, as long the quoted material is brief.

file sharing The ability to transmit or share files over the internet or over computer networks.

flaming Hostile or insulting interactions that people can have on the internet, usually initiated to draw a reaction from someone.

honor system A way of doing something—such as sharing public resources like computers or Wi-Fi—that relies on the honesty of the users, rather than strict rules and surveillance.

hotspot A public place that offers free or conditional Wi-Fi to customers or the general public.

internet predator Someone who uses emails or websites to reach people for the purpose of doing harm to them.

netiquette The manners used while working online.

paraphrase To rewrite another's text or content in one's own words.

plagiarism The act of taking credit for work created by someone else, or using their work without proper attribution.

piggybacking Logging onto an unauthorized Wi-Fi network.

professional correspondence A written letter or email that deals with official business, such as an invitation to a guest speaker.

social networking The practice of reaching out and staying in touch with others.

text A written, digital correspondence sent via signals from one device to another.

Wi-Fi Refers to a wireless internet connection or service.

FOR MORE INFORMATION

Canadian Centre for Child Protection, Inc.
615 Academy Road
Winnipeg, MB R3N 0E7
Canada
(204) 945-5735
(800) 532-9135
Websites: http://www.protectchildren.ca/app/en
The Canadian Centre for Child Protection is a non-profit, charitable
    organization dedicated to the personal safety of all children. Its
    goal is to reduce child victimization by providing programs and
    services to the Canadian public. It operates Cybertip.ca, Canada's
    national tipline for reporting online sexual exploitation of children.
    It is part of the national government's efforts to make Canada safer
    for its citizens.

Family Online Safety Institute
400 7th Street NW, Suite 506
Washington, DC 20004
(202) 775-0158
Website: http://www.fosi.org
Facebook: @FamOnlineSafety
Twitter: @FOSI
The Family Online Safety Institute is an international, nonprofit organization
    that works to develop a safer internet for children and families. It works
    to influence public policies and educate the public.

Internet Education Foundation
1634 I Street, NW, Suite 1100
Washington, DC, 20006

(202) 637-0968
Website: http://neted.org
The Internet Education Foundation is a non-profit organization dedicated to
    informing the public about internet education.

i-Safe Inc.
6189 El Camino Real, Suite 201
Carlsbad, CA 92009
(760) 603-7911
Website: http://www.isafe.org
Twitter: @iSAFEVentures
Instagram: @ idrive_live
Founded in 1998, i-SAFE Inc. is a leader in internet safety education. It is a
    non-profit foundation whose mission is to educate and empower youth
    to make their internet experiences safe and responsible.

Megan Meier Foundation
515 Jefferson, Suite A
St. Charles, MO 63301
(636) 757-3501
E-mail: info@meganmeierfoundation.org
Website: http://www.meganmeierfoundation.org
Twitter: @MeganMeierFndn
Instagram: @meganmeierfoundation
Founded in 2007 by the mother of a cyberbullying victim, the Megan
    Meier Foundation is a global bullying and cyberbullying prevention
    foundation. The organization holds numerous events and
    leads several programs aimed to combat cyberbullying and help
    prevent suicide.

Public Safety Canada
Attn: Public Safety Portal - SafeCanada.ca
269 Laurier Avenue West
Ottawa, ON K1A 0P8
Canada
(800) 755-7047
Website: http://www.safecanada.ca/topic_e.asp?category=3
SafeCanada is part of the Canadian government's online efforts to make
    Canada a safe place for all its citizens wherever they are, including
    when they go online.

Websites

Due to the changing nature of internet links, Rosen Publishing has developed an online list of websites related to the subject of this book. This site is updated regularly. Please use this link to access this list:

http://www.rosenlinks.com/DIL/Net

FOR FURTHER READING

Boyd, Danah. *It's Complicated: The Social Lives of Networked Teens*. New Haven, CT: Yale University Press, 2015.

Cosson, M.J. *The Smart Kid's Guide to Using the Internet*. North Mankato, MN: The Child's World, 2014.

Culp, Jennifer. *Online Gaming Safety and Privacy* (21st Century Safety and Privacy). New York, NY: Rosen Publishing, 2013.

Furgang, Adam. *Searching Online for Image, Audio, and Video Files* (Digital and information Literacy). New York, NY: Rosen Publishing, 2009.

Gaines, Ann. *Ace Your Internet Research* (Ace It! Information Literacy Series). Berkeley Heights, NJ: Enslow Publishers, 2009.

Hinduja, Sameer K., and Justin W. Patchin. *Bullying Beyond the Schoolyard: Preventing and Responding to Cyberbullying*. Thousand Oaks, CA: Corwin, 2014.

Hubbard, Ben. *Staying Safe Online*. North Mankato, MN: Capstone Press, 2017.

Kowalski, Robin. *Cyberbullying: Bullying in the Digital Age*. Hoboken, NJ: Wiley-Blackwell, 2012.

Miles, Lisa. *How to Survive Online Embarassment* (Girl Talk). New York, NY: Rosen Publishing, 2013.

Rustad, Martha E.H. *Learning About Privacy*. Mankato, MN: Capstone Press, 2015.

Sommers, Michael. *The Dangers of Online Predators*. New York, NY: Rosen Central, 2008.

Zuchora-Walske, Christine. *How Can I Be a Good Digital Citizen?* Minneapolis, MN: Lerner Publishing Group, 2016.

BIBLIOGRAPHY

Cox, Amy. "Where are your High-Tech Manners?" CNN, July 3, 2007. http://www.cnn.com/2007/TECH/ptech/07/01/la.tech.manners/index. html?iref=newssearch.

"Cyber Bullying: Statistics and Tips." iSafe.org. Retrieved October 10, 2009 http://www.isafe.org/channels/sub. php?ch=op&sub_id=media_cyber_bullying.

Dean, Katie. "School Blocks Out File-Trading." *Wired*, May 2, 2003. http://www.wired.com/entertainment/music/ news/2003/05/58698.

Kallos, Judith. *Email Etiquette Made Easy*. Raleigh, NC: Lulu.com, 2007.

Marklein, Mary Beth. "Students Aren't using Info Technology Responsibly." USA Today, November 9, 2003. http://www.usatoday.com/news/ education/2003-11-09-students-it_x.htm.

Martin, Jennifer. "$1.9 Million Verdict for Illegal Music Downloads." *Commercial Law*, August 1, 2009. http://ucclaw.blogspot. com/2009/06/19-million-verdict-for-illegal-music.html.

"Parents: Cyber Bullying Led to Teen's Suicide." ABC News, November 19, 2007. http://abcnews.go.com/GMA/ story?id=3882520&page=1.

Shea, Virginia. "The Core Rules of Netiquette." Albion.com. Retrieved May 14, 2009. http://www.albion.com/netiquette/corerules.html.

Shipley, David, and Will Schwalbe. *Send: Why People Email So Badly and How to Do It Better*, Revised Edition. New York, NY: Borzoi Books, 2008.

"Shocking Statistics." SentryPC.com. Retrieved October 10, 2009 (http:// www.sentrypc.com/statistics.htm).

Strawbridge, Matthew. *Netiquette: Internet Etiquette in the Age of the Blog*. Ely, England: Software Reference Ltd., 2006.

Swartz, Jon. "Schoolyard Bullies Get Nastier Online." *USA Today*. March 6, 2005. http://www.usatoday.com/tech/news/2005-03-06-cover-cyberbullies_x.htm.

Vaisman, Mauro. "Facebook, Twitter, and Online Bullying." *Business Week*, March 24, 2009. http://www.businessweek.com/careers/workingparents/blog/archives/2009/03/facebook_twitte.html.

Willard, Nancy. *Cyberbullying and Cyberthreats: Responding to the Challenge of Online Social Aggression, Threats, and Distress.* Champaign, IL: Research Press, 2007.

INDEX

About the Author

Kathy Furgang has been writing books for students for over ten years. She has written several books for children and teens, including nonfiction books about science, technology, and the environment. She worked for eight years as an editor of science textbooks for children and teachers. She lives in upstate New York with her husband and two sons.

Photo Credits

Cover, p. 1 (far left) arek_malang/Shutterstock.com, cover, p. 1 (center left), p. 5 Rawpixel.com/Shutterstock.com; cover, p. 1 (center right, far right) Mediaphotos/Shutterstock.com, Alexey Boldin/Shutterstock.com; p. 8 Ditty_about_summer/Shutterstock.com; p. 9 asiseeit/E+/Getty Images; pp. 10-11 StNewton/Shutterstock.com; p. 14 Flashpop/Stone/Getty Images; p. 17 Robert Daly/OJO Images/Getty Images; p. 20 sturti/E+/Getty Images; p. 24 Ed Bock/Corbis/Getty Images; p. 25 Pixel 4 Images/Shutterstock.com; p. 27 Hero Images/Getty Images; p. 31 Monkey Business Images/Shutterstock.com; p. 33 © iStockphoto.com/digitalskillet; p. 35 Highwaystarz-Photography/iStock/Thinkstock; p. 36 DGLimages/iStock/Thinkstock; cover and interior pages (pixels) © iStockphoto.com/suprun.

Design: Nicole Russo-Duca; Layout: Raúl Rodriguez; Editor: Phil Wolny; Photo Research: Karen Huang